BATTING SECRETS
OF THE
MAJOR LEAGUERS

This is *the* guide for all you ballplayers and future major leaguers. Here are hitting hints from some of the biggest names in professional baseball. Learn the secrets of hitters such as Sal Bando, Bobby Murcer, Lou Piniella, and Bob Bailor, Eric Soderholm, Roy White, and Jim Sundberg. Find out how to select the right bat and the best stance, where the strike zone is, how to meet the ball, how to bunt, and much more.

As an added bonus, Charley Lau, veteran player and batting coach for the New York Yankees, gives introductory tips on hitting, concentration, and everything else you need to know to swing like a pro.

So, grab a copy of *Batting Secrets of the Major Leaguers* and come out swinging!

Batting Secrets of the Major Leaguers

Compiled by **Martin Appel**

Julian Messner New York

Manufactured in the United States of America.
Design by Philip Jaget

Also available in Wanderer Paperback Edition.

Library of Congress Cataloging in Publication Data

Main entry under title:

Batting secrets of the major leaguers.

   SUMMARY: A compilation of tips on batting,
including gripping the bat, learning the strike zone,
bunting, concentrating, and hitting for power.
   1. Batting (Baseball)—Juvenile literature.
[1. Batting (Baseball) 2. Baseball] I. Appel,
Martin.
GV869.B33   1981   796.357′26   80-13709
ISBN 0-671-41315-5

To Brian

Acknowledgments

Special thanks to all the players who consented to lend their time and thoughts, and also to Mike Levanthal and Jim Ogle.

Contents

Introduction

A Batting Coach Speaks Out

Charley Lau is one of the most respected batting instructors currently practicing his art. He has been the batting coach for the Baltimore Orioles, Oakland A's, Kansas City Royals, and New York Yankees. If he ever needed references to get a job—which he doesn't—a young army of players would go to bat for him.

Just as you don't have to be a Hall of Famer to be a great manager, neither do you have to be a batting champion to be an outstanding teacher. Lau, playing eleven years in the major leagues, hit .255, which means he was 52 hits from a .300 lifetime mark.

Lau has very definite ideas about batting and, more importantly, the ability to put them across to a pupil. He is tireless when he finds an eager pupil.

I could lecture on hitting and all the ramifications for a week. As a coach I always try to be positive and never take a negative view of anything. I am sure that there is no hitting problem that can't be worked out. There is a solution to everything, and you must instill that in your mind.

New York Yankees

Charley Lau is considered the finest
hitting instructor in baseball today.

If you have talent, there's a way of uncovering it. If
you dedicate yourself to the task at hand, then there is
no reason why you can't improve. Remember, there is
a solution to every problem, and hard work and dedication will find it.

I have worked with players like Reggie Jackson, Joe
Rudi, Sal Bando, Hal McRae, Amos Otis, Thurman
Munson, Brooks Robinson, and Boog Powell. Here is
some of the advice I have passed along over the years:

It is difficult to talk about the task of selecting a bat,
but you should be concerned more with length than
with weight. A mere half inch is very critical, and if
you pick a bat just that much too long, you will hurt
your hitting.

For example, Reggie Jackson used to swing a 36- or
35½-inch bat, but he switched to 34 inches and that
has helped him. You must have the proper length to
assure that you get the bat head on the ball at just the
right time consistently. Sure, a 90-foot bat would en-
able you to hit a ball 90 miles—if you could get it
around at the right instant.

Forget that old saying that practice makes perfect—that's nonsense. But a perfect practice can lead you toward perfection. You improve through repetition, doing it over and over again. Getting consistent strikes in batting practice is very important.

Don't waste a single swing of batting practice. It isn't a time for fooling around; it is a time for practice, practice, and more practice. Learn to use the bat skillfully while you are taking batting practice. Play mental games, set up different situations, and try to execute what you think the situation would require.

Batting practice is a time to learn to go with the pitch, to try hitting to all fields, to have a purpose on each swing, and to keep repeating, since repetition is the best teacher. At the same time, if the pitcher isn't throwing strikes, don't swing. That could get you into bad habits.

There is no moment more important in the life of a hitter than the moments he spends observing the pitcher before going to bat. It is a time for analyzing what is in the pitcher's mind, noting how he performs on the mound, and seeing what his best pitch is on this given day. If you are a left-handed hitter and the pitcher is a right-handed sinker-ball artist, plan how you are going to battle him. Are you going to try to pull him or are you going to try to hit up the middle?

Have a purpose in mind before you get to the plate. What is the situation? With two on and none out, for example, you must think of advancing the runners. That is your primary objective, not getting a hit. With men on second and third, none out, and the infield back, you have to hit to the right side. That scores one and puts the other on third.

Most of you young players don't think about this. You think you must go up swinging for a base hit. A pop out does nothing, but a ground ball to the right side will advance runners.

I think one of the most overrated items of batting instruction is the grip. It is difficult for anyone to teach you the proper grip, since every batter is different. As you seek the best grip for you, remember two things:

1. *Find the grip that makes your hands the most flexible. The more freedom of movement you have in your hands, the better you can adjust to any pitch.*
2. *The most important thing about finding your grip is to remove tension. Anything you can do to take tension away helps, as tension destroys a hitter.*

When we come to finding the proper stance, we are in another area, and hours could be spent discussing it. In this I always try to relate to golfers, since alignment of your body is very important. I am a great believer in the parallel or square stance, where you have everything in balance and develop rhythm.

Preparatory stance is very important. Find a balanced position first, a position where you have your body under control. Square your feet, then start moving in rhythm, and go on from there. I think a hitter should always be moving at the plate, not standing still. I believe if you are moving when you get your pitch, you will be moving from a moving start.

What is the right stance? How close do you stand to the plate? How far do you stand from the plate? How close or how far should you be from the pitcher? One answer covers all these questions for the moment: Use the rule of thumb, but then expand.

Against a pitcher who can really throw, stand as deep as possible in the batter's box. Against a breaking-ball pitcher, move up as far as you can. Eighty out of a hundred hitters will be near the middle of the plate when they strike. Find a happy medium by trial and error, then stick with what's best for you.

Remember that to swing properly you must be able to extend your arms. For that reason I do not advocate standing close to the plate, or, as we say, crowding the plate. Doing that I believe will force you into bad habits over the long run. Sure, you can do it now and then in your ever-running battle with pitchers, but you are better off if you don't crowd the plate.

I believe in a short stride, and that's the first thing I look for in a hitter. You can't teach a short stride, but it is a good thing to have. I also look for aggressiveness toward the pitcher; a hitter has to challenge the pitcher.

If you keep telling a youngster to take a short stride, you get him thinking the wrong way and take away his aggressiveness. So let him adjust normally. A positive pass at the pitcher is the key. If you try to concentrate on teaching him a short stride, you won't get good results.

Now we come to a very important asset: knowing where the strike zone is. It's tough to learn, and there are no shortcuts. Only repetition and good batting practice pitchers who consistently throw strikes can help you with this time-consuming task.

Actually, I believe a major league hitter is born with a good knowledge of the strike zone. Although it can be polished through batting practice, a Ted Williams-type knowledge of the strike zone is a gift.

Advancing the runner is the issue that has caused me to get fired once or twice. I am a firm believer that all right-handed hitters should learn to hit to right in order to advance a runner. I don't care who the hitter is or how good he may be, I still think there are times when being able to advance the runner is a great asset. You win by advancing runners, so a right-hander must learn to hit to right, and a left-handed swinger must pull the ball.

Free-swinging home-run hitters who strike out a lot are a liability in this department. When any hitter strikes out with a man on base, his turn at bat was a complete failure. However, a little ground ball to advance the base runner would have made it a success.

We are always looking for the perfect swing, but do you know how rare that is? A good hitter will go to bat 500 times a year and might have 1,200 swings, of which 75 could be considered good and only about 50 could be rated perfect. That should help you realize just how tough hitting really is.

When you speak of power, you open up a broad statement and a wide field. Basically, if you are strong, you hit for power. But if you aren't strong, you aren't a power hitter.

If you are a little guy, don't despair. That doesn't mean you can't hit for distance. All you have to do is put it all together in proper sequence—balance, rhythm, stride, and transfer of weight. Then hit the ball at the proper point of contact. If a little guy does all that, he'll hit a ball that carries. He has executed the perfect swing, which doesn't happen often. In other words, if you put it all into perfect sequence you'll hit it well.

The key to bunting is getting yourself in the proper position at the right time to bunt the ball. There is a little fear in most bunters, but that's not their main problem. The problems are varied: being caught late or caught moving so you aren't in position when the ball arrives. You must also be balanced perfectly.

To be a successful bunter you must concentrate on the angle of the bat head. It should always be a little above parallel. Balance in getting into position to bunt is equally important.

A new term has come into baseball in the past ten years—designated hitter. It is a tough job for anyone, but the most successful DH is an older player willing to accept the role. A DH has to learn to take care of himself, practice properly, and think like a DH. In between times at bat, he should observe the pitcher and his sequences. It is harder to stay in condition as a DH than as an everyday player, so conditioning is important.

The same ideas work for a pinch hitter, too. You have to prepare differently than a player who plays every day. You must really study pitchers, especially relief pitchers. A man who pinch-hits a great deal should have all relievers cataloged. What does he throw? How does he work on a hitter? What does he throw in certain situations? If you know the pitchers and their style, you will be a good pinch hitter.

Is there a most important thing in hitting? If there is, it has to be seeing the ball and watching it. It's safe to say that the good hitter sees the ball longer than the less successful hitters.

To be a good hitter there must be a lack of tension; you must have rhythm and you must be concerned with bat position. The bat has to get to a certain spot at a certain moment and within an area of one inch. Concentration is a broad term, but one application for a good hitter is his ability to be able to swing without turning his head, thus keeping his eye on the ball.

Work as many hours as it takes to get proper weight

shift as you move into the ball. You must discipline that sort of movement in your head, think of it until you can do it automatically.

I hope you'll find all of this helpful. Although the written word is a great means of communicating, you can't beat getting out there on the field and playing. Just remember, for every problem there is a solution. All it takes is hard work.

Good luck!

Charley Lau

1.

Meet the Panel

As you will soon discover, there is not always a right way and a wrong way to hit. Different ideas will work better for different people.

Many people have said that hitting a baseball is the hardest thing to do in all sports. The art of hitting a round, spinning, moving object that is coming from only 60½ feet away at speeds of up to 100 miles per hour with a thin wooden bat is hard to match. In golf, the ball is sitting still. In tennis, you've got a large hitting surface. But in baseball, it sure isn't easy.

The best hitter who ever lived, Ty Cobb, had a terrific lifetime batting average of .367. This means that the best hitter in the game didn't get a hit about 63 times out of every 100 he went to bat. So obviously, no one has ever come up with a way to bat 1.000. There just *isn't* a way.

The stars in this book have all been successful as hitters, but they come in all sizes and strengths and have to make adjustments to suit their own games. Being ready to face those adjustments is very important. If you're smaller than the big home-run hitters, you'll never be successful if you think you can copy them.

Even hitters of the same size have different opinions on what to do, as you will see. That doesn't mean that one is right and one is wrong. It only means that everyone has to find out what's right for him.

Read this book for pleasure as much as for instruction. Too much advice, particularly if it's all different, can really put you in a frustrated mess. You can use this book in different ways to help you.

One way would be to pick out a hitter you think might be like you. Try out what he says and see how it works. If it all seems to work well except for one or two areas, try someone else on those subjects. Maybe they can pass on a tip that will help you.

You could also read what everyone has to say on a certain subject and make a choice from among them. You'll often see most people agreeing on something. But one or two usually feel otherwise, and maybe they're the ones best suited to your style.

You have plenty of time to develop the style most comfortable to you. Even big leaguers are often making changes during their careers. So don't feel you have to pick a certain stance or grip because your favorite player likes it. It may not be right for you.

The following players have offered their experience and advice for this book:

Toronto Blue Jays

Bob Bailor:

Bob was the Most Valuable Player on the Toronto Blue Jays in both of the Jays' first two seasons. Bob is right-handed, stands 5'11", and weighs 170 pounds. He plays the outfield and the infield and has always been more of a singles and doubles hitter than a long-ball hitter.

Milwaukee Brewers

Sal Bando:

Sal was the captain of the Oakland A's, the three-time World Champions of the early 1970s, and he earned a reputation for great leadership. Sal is a right-handed third baseman, is 6' tall, and weighs 205 pounds. He has good power and is a terrific run producer.

Atlanta Braves

Jeff Burroughs:

Jeff has been a home-run star in both the American and National leagues. He first played in the major leagues when he was only nineteen years old. Jeff is 6'2" and weighs 195 pounds. He wears glasses. He's mostly found playing the outfield and is a right-handed hitter.

Montreal Expos

Dave Cash:

Dave led the National League in times at bat for three consecutive seasons and, in 1975, set an all-time record with 699 at bats. He rarely draws walks and hits many singles, doubles, and triples. He's a second baseman who stands 6' tall and weighs 175 pounds. Dave is a right-handed hitter.

Kansas City Royals

Hal McRae:

Hal has played for championship teams in both Cincinnati and Kansas City. He hit an amazing 54 doubles in 1977 for the Royals, serving mostly as a designated hitter. Hal is right-handed, stands 5'11", and weighs 180 pounds.

Pittsburgh Pirates

John Milner:

John spent the first portion of his career with the New York Mets, where he set new team home run records for left-handed hitters. John, an outfielder and first baseman, is 6' and weighs 185 pounds.

New York Yankees

Bobby Murcer:
Bobby has been one of baseball's most consistent run producers over the last ten years. He hits with good power and is also a fine outfielder with good speed. Bobby is left-handed, stands 5'11", and weighs 180 pounds.

Baltimore Orioles

Eddie Murray:
Eddie was Rookie of the Year with the Baltimore Orioles in 1977, hitting with more power than he had ever shown in the minor leagues. Eddie, an outfielder and first baseman, is a switch hitter. He is 6'2" and weighs 190 pounds.

Texas Rangers

Al Oliver:
Al has been one of baseball's best hitters since 1969, when he came up with the Pittsburgh Pirates. He's been a runner-up in the batting race in both leagues. He is an outfielder who bats left, stands 6' tall, and weighs 195 pounds.

New York Yankees

Lou Piniella:

Lou has a reputation for never being satisfied with himself, even though he's usually a .300 hitter. He has been a star with both the Royals and the Yankees. Lou, an outfielder, is 6'2", weighs 190 pounds, and is right-handed.

Boston Red Sox

Jerry Remy:

Jerry is a singles hitter who came up through the California Angels organization. He had three .300 seasons in the minors. Jerry is a second baseman who bats left, stands 5'9", and weighs 165 pounds.

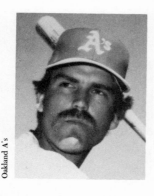

Oakland A's

Dave Revering:

Dave is a first baseman who spent eight years in the minor leagues before being traded to Oakland from Cincinnati. He has always had good power and a high batting average. Dave is 6'4", weighs 210 pounds, and bats left-handed.

Pittsburgh Pirates

Bill Robinson:

It took Bill many years to become a great hitter, proving the value of patience and hard work. Nine minor league seasons and three years in the American League led to success at last in the National League. Bill is right-handed, stands 6'2", and weighs 200 pounds. He's an outfielder.

St. Louis Cardinals

Ted Simmons:

Ted has been one of the best catchers in baseball for many years, with a lifetime .300 batting average and good power. He is a switch hitter who stands 5'11" and weighs a solid 195 pounds. He needed only three years in the minor leagues.

Chicago White Sox

Eric Soderholm:

Eric missed an entire season with an injury and still came back as a fine hitter with even more power than he had shown before. Eric is a third baseman who stands 6' tall, weighs 187 pounds, and bats right-handed.

Texas Rangers

Jim Sundberg:

Jim reached the major leagues after only one season in the minors and raised his batting average almost 100 points between 1975 and 1977. Jim, a catcher, is right-handed, stands 6' tall, and weighs 190 pounds.

Houston Astros

Bob Watson:

Bob is one of the most consistent players in the major leagues, with a lifetime average of .300. He is a fine run producer and team leader. Bob, who mostly plays first base, is right-handed, stands 6'1½", and weighs 201 pounds.

New York Yankees

Roy White:

Roy is among the steadiest of all baseball performers over the years. He is a consistent switch-hitter who combines durability and speed for success. He is an outfielder who stands 5'10" and weighs 171 pounds.

Minnesota Twins

Butch Wynegar:
Butch was the American League Rookie of the Year in 1976 as a catcher with the Minnesota Twins. He is mostly a singles hitter but can hit the long ball on occasion too. Butch is a switch-hitter who stands 6'1" and weighs 190 pounds.

2.

Selecting the Right Bat

As any Little Leaguer knows, there are different sizes of bats available—different in weight and in length. In the major leagues, there are even a lot of different shapes—some with thin handles, some with no knobs on the bottom, and some even cupped at the tip, curving into the bat. Players order dozens of bats at a time and are always trying new ones out.

SAL BANDO: I use every style and weight there is because there are times I feel stronger than I do at other times. If I'm facing an off-speed pitcher, I'll use a lighter bat because you have to wait longer and then whip the bat around faster. Against a hard thrower like Ron Guidry or Rich Gossage, I'll use a heavier bat—you don't have to hit the ball as hard or move the bat so far.

JIM SUNDBERG: You've got to use a bat that's comfortable for you—not a bat that someone else on your team uses or the bat some other good hitter uses. I usually move to a lighter bat as the season goes on because I seem to get it around better.

EDDIE MURRAY: I use a pretty light bat—35 inches and 32 ounces. I usually swing with my wrists so the ball jumps off the bat well.

Eddie Murray gets his power from his wrists and uses a rather light bat to generate speed.

BOB WATSON: I've used the heaviest bat in the majors over the last seven or eight years—42 ounces. It's just right for my kind of contact swing. I'm not really looking for bat speed; I'm looking for density. I get jammed a lot on pitches, and with the heavy bat, I can still pop one over the infield.

HAL McRAE: You've got to make sure you've got the strike zone covered, so don't cheat yourself on length.

11

ERIC SODERHOLM: My high school coach told me, "Find a bat that you like—and marry it!" If you change bats a lot, you confuse your pattern. Even if you go into a slump, don't change bats.

DAVE REVERING: I'll use different bats for different pitchers. If a guy is overpowering, like a Ron Guidry, I'll use a lighter bat to get around quicker.

BILL ROBINSON: A bat's like a part of you. It's almost like taking your wife or child up to the plate. I've used the same style for six or seven years now, although Dave Parker and Willie Stargell have almost convinced me to go to a heavier bat. But I've always preferred a skinny handle and skinny barrel to give me maximum bat speed.

BOBBY MURCER: Balance is very important to me. I don't like a bat that feels too top-heavy. I use a medium handle with a large barrel. But the important thing for anyone is just to have it feel right in your hands.

LOU PINIELLA: My hands aren't particularly large, so I prefer a thin handle on the bat. The weight is pretty light for me. I start the season at around 32 ounces and then drop an ounce or two as the season drags on.

BOB BAILOR: Come August or September, I like to drop down to a thinner handle. At that point, my wrists can take over and do more of the work for me.

JEFF BURROUGHS: I use a 34-inch, 32-ounce bat, which is considered pretty light for a power hitter. If

Ted Simmons uses batting practice to get loose. If he's in a slump, he devotes hours of hard work to it.

the ball has good wood in it though, and if it jumps off the bat well, I wouldn't care if it weighed 10 ounces!

TED SIMMONS: I've moved upward in bat weight over the years. I'm at 35 inches and 33½ ounces now and can swing just as aggressively as years ago. The more weight there is, the harder the ball is going to be hit if you can do everything else the same.

ROY WHITE: A switch-hitter should recognize his different strengths and weaknesses from opposite sides of the plate and select a bat accordingly. Just because your arms may look and feel equally strong, there may be an adjustment required. Most switch-hitters have more power from one side.

3.

Batting Practice

Back in 1927 when the Yankees were known as "Murderer's Row," they faced the Pittsburgh Pirates in the World Series. Before the first game, during batting practice, Babe Ruth, Lou Gehrig, and all those great sluggers hit ball after ball into the stands. The Pirates were so impressed—even a little frightened some said—that they lost four straight games.

Batting practice can be used to put on a good show for the fans or perhaps to scare the other team a little. But it's also a chance to practice for the game. Some players take BP more seriously than others, but no one can afford to ignore it.

AL OLIVER: Batting practice to me is a chance to practice game situations. I hit the ball just as I would during a game. If the pitch is away from me, I'll hit it to the opposite field. If it's inside, I'll pull it. Trying to hit home runs during batting practice is a "no-no."

SAL BANDO: I always try to just make good contact with the ball. I like to hit the ball to the opposite field. Pulling the ball will come naturally during the game—I work on just getting the bat on the ball during BP.

JIM SUNDBERG: Batting practice is very important to me. It's the best time to improve yourself as a hitter. You've always got to work at anything to improve—even when I'm catching I try to improve. If you develop the right attitude toward these things, everything will come more naturally.

BUTCH WYNEGAR: It's a funny thing, but I think that when I hit the ball well in batting practice I have a bad game and vice versa. So I try not to think too much in the batting cage. I just try to get loose and make sure I'm seeing the ball well.

EDDIE MURRAY: I don't take batting practice too seriously; I just try to get loose. I don't really bear down. If a left-hander is going to be starting the game, I'll bat right-handed in BP, but that's about as seriously as I'll take it. One thing though—if I'm in a slump, I'll come out to the park early and take *serious* batting practice!

DAVE REVERING: You've got to take it seriously. It's part of your job. I'll always pretend I'm hitting in a game situation.

HAL McRAE: If you're going to take BP, do it right. You can develop bad habits otherwise.

ERIC SODERHOLM: Whatever you do in batting practice will carry over into a game. I prefer live pitching to a pitching machine, so I take batting practice as often as I can off the real thing.

BOB WATSON: I really don't take batting practice except for spring training, the off-season, and the first two or three weeks of the season. I find that the pitches in batting practice are at only about half-speed, so it makes me do things incorrectly. I know the fans like to come and watch the players take BP, but for me, it's obsolete. I'll only do it during the summer if I want to test the background in a new park.

LOU PINIELLA: The first few swings, I just like to get loose. Then I'll go to work on what I'm trying to accomplish that night, depending on who's pitching. I use batting practice to work out bad habits whenever possible.

BILL ROBINSON: In seventeen years, I haven't missed batting practice more than once or twice. If I can correct something during batting practice, it sure is better than working on it during a game. Of course, it's a better opportunity to experiment, too. And if I'm hitting good during practice, it helps get me mentally psyched up for the game.

BOBBY MURCER: To tell the truth, if you haven't gotten your swing down by July or August, you're in a lot of trouble, batting practice or not. I just use it as a little tune-up.

JERRY REMY: I'll start off hitting ten balls to left field, then ten up the middle, and then I'll pull ten to right. Batting practice helps develop discipline and concentration.

TED SIMMONS: Unless I'm in a slump, I just use batting practice to get loose. But if I'm doing poorly, I like to get out to the park maybe six hours early and have someone throw to me for about a half hour, uninterrupted. It's a chance to get that good feeling back.

JOHN MILNER: I use batting practice to get into the right frame of mind—to get loose and get the timing down in my hands and wrists. Just try to see the ball properly. Don't think in terms of game situations.

BOB BAILOR: It rains so often in Toronto that we miss batting practice a lot, and that bothers me. When you're in a groove, you don't like to upset the rhythm. When I'm taking BP, I'll usually bunt a few and then try to go to the opposite field.

JEFF BURROUGHS: Batting practice is one of the really fun parts of the game. All that good spirit around the batting cage really makes you enjoy being a baseball player. I hardly ever miss it!

ROY WHITE: I take an equal number of swings righty and lefty because a relief pitcher can force you to change during the game and you want to be ready. I like to concentrate on timing and the hand-eye coordination.

4.

Waiting in the
On Deck Circle

A lot of hitters spend time in the on deck circle rubbing the bat with pine tar, swinging weighted bats, or adjusting the helmet. Did you ever notice that some of the best hitters just kneel down and watch the pitcher? You can learn a lot that way.

DAVE CASH: There should be a lot of things on your mind in the on deck circle. What part of the game are you in? What might you be called upon to do? I try to see if the pitcher might be tipping something off in his delivery. I watch the defense too—an infielder may be moving to his left or the center fielder may be moving on a certain kind of pitch.

BUTCH WYNEGAR: I often watch to see how they're pitching to my teammate Roy Smalley because they often pitch to me the same way. I try to see what a pitcher might have going for him. But you've got to do this throughout the game, not just on deck. I like to talk to the guys on the bench who've batted before me to see what the pitcher is throwing.

SAL BANDO: I think about how the pitcher has pitched to me in the past. Then I'll concentrate on the angle or the position he's letting the ball come from—especially if I haven't faced him before. In the on deck circle, try to zero in on anything that you can possibly pick up!

AL OLIVER: I don't concentrate so much on how he's working on another hitter. I'm more interested in what kind of fastball he happens to have that day.

JIM SUNDBERG: Back in college, every pitcher you saw was new. In the major leagues, things are a little easier because you face the same people again and again. But when someone new comes along, you've really got to study him. Look for that release point. Where is the ball coming from? I want to know if his curveball breaks slowly or sharply.

ERIC SODERHOLM: For me, it's a chance to practice the art of crystallized thinking. I'm on deck, but I can actually see the pitcher throwing to me. I haven't refined this yet, but it's very mental and very effective.

BOB WATSON: I don't study the pitcher only from the on deck circle. I watch him from the bench, and I'll even walk out to the visitor's bullpen before the game and try to watch him warm up.

DAVE REVERING: Without many veterans on our club, you really couldn't pick up advice, so it was all "see and learn" for me.

BOBBY MURCER: I like to know what a pitcher's best pitch is. If he's got you in trouble when you're up, that's the pitch to watch for.

BILL ROBINSON: It seems the newer pitchers always give us trouble, so you've really got to study them carefully and get any edge you can. I keep a book on all the National League pitchers, and I'm always looking for that point of delivery. In fact, I cut a pitcher in half in my mind and only see the side of his body the ball is coming from.

LOU PINIELLA: There are usually one or two hitters in the lineup who bat exactly like you or close to it. So I especially study how they're being pitched to. I want to know what pitches are working for the pitcher that day. If his curveballs are bouncing in the dirt, wait for the fastball.

JOHN MILNER: A pitcher won't pitch everyone the same, so observing from the on deck circle may not tell you what kind of pitching you'll see. But still, you get a chance to pick up the rhythm of the pitcher.

JEFF BURROUGHS: I'm not one of those who keep little notebooks on how pitchers pitch me, but I've got a good memory for it. On the Braves, we had video cassettes for us to study the pitchers and refresh our memories before we hit.

BOB BAILOR: I always check the newspapers to see who's pitching, and they're usually right. From that moment on, I'm going through how they pitch me in my mind.

5.

Gripping the Bat

Golfers seem to spend a lot of time adjusting their grips, but it can be just as important in baseball. Ty Cobb was famous for holding his hands apart on the bat handle, but today, almost every player holds his hands together.

EDDIE MURRAY: When I was younger, I held my hands so low on the bat that I actually had a hand around the knob. But that grip didn't last long—it gave me blisters. Now I use a bat without a knob, and I feel really comfortable holding my hands all the way down at the bottom of the bat.

SAL BANDO: I like to cradle the bat in my hands and to hold the bat fairly loose. You shouldn't try to squeeze sawdust out of it! When you make contact with the ball, you will naturally tighten your grip.

BUTCH WYNEGAR: It can get so cold in Minnesota sometimes that I'll have to wear a glove on my hand. But I'm really not happy about it. I like to feel the bat in my hand. And I'll use pine tar to make the bat sticky and give me an even better grip.

DAVE CASH: Like selecting a bat, a grip is a very individual thing. I try to place the bat on the finger part of my hand, not the tips. It seems to make my wrists react more quickly. I like pine tar or resin, and I'll wear a glove when it's cold.

HAL McRAE: I like to hold the bat in my fingers, not near the back of my hand. Do that, and you'll get a bone bruise.

BOB WATSON: Pick up the bat and line the knuckles up evenly. Some guys roll the top hand over, but not me. I like to wear a glove, too. When you swing the bat 600 times in the regular season and another 2,000 in spring training, your hands can take a real beating.

JERRY REMY: I don't even know where my fingers are in relationship to the bat. I just pick it up and let it feel comfortable. I'll choke it up a little.

LOU PINIELLA: I like to get the handle well into my fingertips. Gripping that way gives me better bat speed, and my wrists seem to break faster.

TED SIMMONS: You want to keep those hands just comfortably loose until the moment of impact. Then nature takes over.

ROY WHITE: There have been times when I've found myself gripping the bat too tightly—and that's a message to me to relax a little more.

6.

Selecting a Comfortable Stance

It's hard to find two hitters with the same stance. No one looked more awkward in his stance than Stan Musial, but he's in the Hall of Fame. Comfort seems to be the whole secret, but there can also be some strategy involved.

AL OLIVER: I used to stand back in the batter's box, but around 1972 I moved up. It seemed to make it easier for me to hit the breaking balls—I was getting a lot of them before they broke. Now, I stand pretty much even with home plate.

BUTCH WYNEGAR: Sometimes in batting practice you might hit upon a stance that feels comfortable. Go ahead and try it! As long as you're comfortable, that's half the battle!

EDDIE MURRAY: I have about four different stances, and I keep switching off. Usually, I'll stand at the back of the batter's box. I may vary, depending on the pitcher. Then again, there are some pitchers I never feel comfortable with!

SAL BANDO: You've got to be comfortable. Forget about copying a Carew or a Jackson or a Mantle. Be yourself and be comfortable!

BOB WATSON: Just be yourself. I stand slightly closed, with my feet shoulder width apart.

DAVE REVERING: I find myself varying a little from pitcher to pitcher, always trying to adjust.

BOBBY MURCER: Just be yourself. If we all imitated, we'd all look like Ted Williams, and I suppose we'd all hit .400.

BILL ROBINSON: I actually take my front foot and draw a line, six to eight inches away, and form an imaginary wall that I don't want to cross.

JERRY REMY: It helps me if I remember to keep my front foot pointed toward the shortshop.

JEFF BURROUGHS: Everyone has a different stance. I seldom stand at the back of the batter's box—I'm usually well up front. But if you watch carefully, I think you'll see that 99 percent of the hitters all wind up looking alike when they make contact.

TED SIMMONS: I really crowd the plate, daring the pitcher to throw at me. If I'm hit, of course, I've got no complaint. But to crowd that plate gives me a really good shot at the outside pitches—I can even pull them.

ROY WHITE: My stance, left-handed especially, really leads into an uncoiling action as the pitch comes in. I have completely different stances righty and lefty, but I've been reasonably steady with them over the years.

7.

Striding

Striding is a natural part of the swing, and shifting your weight forward is what you want to achieve. Mel Ott, a great player for the New York Giants, and Dick McAuliffe, who starred for Detroit not too many years ago, actually lifted their front legs about a foot in the air when they stepped forward. But for the most part, striding is just a natural, smooth step.

DAVE CASH: Sometimes I'll watch myself on films and it doesn't even look like me! But at least I can see if I'm striding properly. I like to stay squared away with my shoulders free, my hands free, and my weight evenly distributed before stepping toward the pitch.

BUTCH WYNEGAR: I know I'm in trouble when I'm overstriding. And when I do that, I can't get around on the pitch as I should. About a fifteen-inch stride is right for me, but it all depends, of course, on how wide you keep your feet apart in your stance. Striding is important for proper weight distribution, but to me, hitting is all in the hands!

BOB WATSON: I actually draw a line in the dirt to remind me not to overstride. I have good balance, and a short, four-to-six-inch stride is right for me.

DAVE REVERING: Most of the good hitters take a very short stride. My own is about six or seven inches.

Bob Bailor tends to stride into the plate rather than toward the pitcher because he starts with a wide-open stance.

HAL McRAE: It helps if you take a positive effort toward the pitcher or toward the base line. Don't overstride.

JERRY REMY: In my stance, I'm pointing toward the shortstop, and that's what I want to do when I stride. I'm a left-handed hitter, and I like to get the ball off in that general direction.

JOHN MILNER: Think of the stride like dancing. It's all part of the rhythm of the game. When I came up with the Mets, Willie Mays pointed out a difference between us. He showed me that I approached the ball with the bottom half of my body, and he did it with the top half. He didn't suggest that I change, but it was an interesting observation.

BOB BAILOR: Because I have an unusual, wide-open stance, I stride toward home plate rather than parallel with it.

Toronto Blue Jays

8.

Concentration

A player's concentration can be the most important part of a game. There are a lot of ways to become distracted during a game, and the best hitters are the ones who have the best concentration.

AL OLIVER: Nothing stops my concentration. A bomb could go off between the mound and home plate, and I'll still hit a line drive somewhere. You can't ever take your eye off the ball. I'm lucky—I've always had this. I think I can hit anyone, and if he gets me out, I give him credit. But if I get a hit off him, I expect that he'll give me credit too!

DAVE CASH: Concentration is hard with all the distractions in a ball park, especially with a big crowd on hand and everyone screaming. You know how fans clap their hands to rattle a pitcher? Hey, that works—and sometimes on a hitter too. I'd say that just before a pitch is delivered is the maximum point of concentration. I'm sure the batter, the catcher, and the pitcher don't hear anything at all.

BUTCH WYNEGAR: Concentration is what this game is all about. But it's hard. I never talk to the catcher or the umpire, and I try not to listen to them either. I don't know if you can ever reach a peak with your concentration, but you've got to keep developing it.

ERIC SODERHOLM: It's not easy, but you've got to try to avoid a case of "rabbit ears"—hearing the fans and everything else around. You've got to get into your own little world.

HAL McRAE: When you don't concentrate, you swing at bad pitches. And that's usually because you're not seeing the full 60 feet of the ball—you're missing the point of release. I'm not always satisfied with my concentration. It's hard to get it right every time.

LOU PINIELLA: Concentration goes along with confidence. If you go to bat knowing that what you're doing is right, you should be OK. I concentrate on the release point of the ball because it's obvious that the longer look you have, the more it is to your advantage. I'll be honest, though, my concentration is not that good. If someone is yelling at me from the dugout or the stands, I hear 'em!

JERRY REMY: After you've said your hellos to the catcher, just stop and *think*. What will the pitcher be throwing me in this situation?

BOB BAILOR: You know, sometimes you'll see a guy call time to get the second-base umpire to move out of the way or to have a piece of paper picked up. That's a guy whose concentration isn't what it should be. I like to think that my level is just where I want it. I won't ever be bothered by the paper or the umpire.

JEFF BURROUGHS: The acquired knowledge of baseball grows into confidence in yourself, and that's what concentration's all about.

TED SIMMONS: It's a whole pattern with me, pitch by pitch. I approach the plate and say to myself, "Who's this pitcher? What has he thrown me before? What has he been throwing others today?" Then I'll take a pitch and step out and say, "What did he throw me? Have I seen it before? What do I want to do with this pitch?" And I'll step back in, and the pattern repeats each time.

ROY WHITE: People tell me I always look too intense on the field, but that's just the way I bear down and concentrate. I don't think you can get too involved in the game unless you start thinking about what other players should be doing and overlook yourself.

9.

Coaching

You're never too old to learn, but good coaching begins as soon as a youngster starts to play. By the time a player reaches the major leagues, he should have his skills fairly well developed, but you can always learn something new.

In the major leagues, there are batting coaches, pitching coaches, and sometimes even baserunning and infield coaches. Often a pitching coach will get a lot of praise when his staff has a good season, but major league coaches are usually in the background and not nearly as well known as the manager or the players.

EDDIE MURRAY: In Baltimore, they teach you how to play the game all over again when you sign with their organization. They stress constant repetition of fundamentals until everything comes automatically during a game.

BUTCH WYNEGAR: I was really set in my ways before I signed to play professional baseball. I had no plans for anyone to change me at all. But in the Minnesota organization, with hitters like Rod Carew and Tony Oliva and a manager like Gene Mauch, a player would have been foolish not to listen to good advice.

AL OLIVER: In the Pittsburgh organization, no one ever interfered with my hitting. That helped me, as it let me continue my positive approach, and my confidence was never hurt. But the Pirates always had such great hitters—like Clemente and Stargell—that I'd watch them on my own to see what I could pick up.

DAVE CASH: I came up through the Pirate organization too, and there was good coaching all the way, with Don Hoak in the minors and Danny Murtaugh in the majors. Danny Ozark at Philadelphia was later a big help to me. I think good coaching is very important at the major league level. The minors are more like a proving ground, weeding out the best prospects.

JIM SUNDBERG: I had only one year in the minors, so I had to pick up a lot of things once I reached the majors. I got a lot just by observing other players. I think really good hitting instructors are very rare—very hard to find.

DAVE REVERING: I was very fortunate to come up through the Cincinnati organization, probably the best in baseball for coaching on the minor league level. Most clubs do things in reverse—they'll have their best coaches in the majors.

HAL McRAE: In the minors, there are usually twenty-five players for one coach, and that's where you really need closer attention. So there's a lot more coaching in the majors than you'd expect, and you get two or three years' worth in the big leagues that you probably should have gotten in the minors.

BOB WATSON: More former major leaguers are getting into college coaching now, and that's good. The quality will improve, and good coaching will start earlier.

ERIC SODERHOLM: This is the biggest problem in professional baseball. Most coaches show you what works for *them*. Very, very few can relate things that will work for *you*.

JERRY REMY: In the minors, there's just not enough time to work with everyone. You've got to remember to hit your own way. Take advice only if you think it directly applies to you. I personally don't like changing, even if I'm slumping.

BOB BAILOR: These days, you can tell the players with college backgrounds even in the minors. They get a better jump on good coaching because there's not enough of it in the minors. It's another good reason to go to college.

JEFF BURROUGHS: Let's face it, if a coach is good, he wants to be in the major leagues and live that good life. It takes a really dedicated instructor to stay in the minors by choice. Most learning is accomplished by watching and talking to other players. I'm still doing those things and still learning today.

ROY WHITE: I've been fortunate to spend most of my career on one team, so I haven't been exposed to the thinking of different organizations much. I think that can confuse you, particularly if someone wants to start all over with your style—which, after all, got you to the big leagues in the first place.

New York Yankees

Roy White felt that he was helped by spending so many seasons with one club. He wasn't confused by different styles between the teams.

10.

Learning the Strike Zone

Yogi Berra was known as a "bad-ball" hitter. That meant he could even get hits on pitches out of the strike zone. Players like him are hard to find. Most major league players will be able to hit all good pitches, as long as they aren't fooled. The thing that separates the great hitters from the rest is the ability to know the strike zone so that you can tell a strike well before it reaches home plate. That gives you, instead of the pitcher, the edge in the duel between the mound and the plate.

DAVE CASH: When you've learned the strike zone—that's when the ball will look like a basketball coming in to you! So big there's no way you can miss it! Learning the strike zone is something you never master—you just try to get better every day.

JIM SUNDBERG: I think umpires respect the judgment of good hitters. On a close pitch, a respected hitter may get the benefit of the doubt. Reputation can be a great thing.

BUTCH WYNEGAR: I'd say a catcher has a little advantage when he comes to bat because he does have a pretty good idea of what the umpire's calling that day. But I'm never going to give the umpire the chance to ring me up. Anything that's close, I'm swinging!

EDDIE MURRAY: The main thing is, you just can't swing at bad pitches. You've always got to try to cut down on this. And the more you cut down, the more the odds come over to your side.

ERIC SODERHOLM: I've got to know the zone where *I* can hit the ball best. The first two strikes are devoted to that. After the second strike is when you have to learn the real strike zone and protect the plate.

BOB WATSON: There's your strike zone and the umpire's. Yours is recognizing your strengths. And the sooner you know where the pitch will be, the better off you will be.

BILL ROBINSON: It takes a rare talent to master the strike zone. I haven't done it—I know that. But I think if you really master it, you lose some of your aggressive quality at the plate. The whole game is this: They throw it, and I hit it. If it's close, I'm going to swing at it.

LOU PINIELLA: I swing at a lot of bad pitches, but I try to avoid the high ones, because you'll usually miss them or pop them up. Some people say you have to adjust from one league to the other, but look at Al Oliver—he didn't have to adjust at all.

BOBBY MURCER: I think they call the inside pitch a strike more often in the National League. You've got to know the umpire, and you can't be over-anx-

Bobby Murcer feels that waiting for his pitch is always worthwhile because sooner or later the pitcher will throw it.

ious. I like to make the pitcher come to me. You figure that one out of every three pitches, at least, is going to be a good pitch to hit.

JERRY REMY: In spring training, Ted Williams told us, "Just swing at strikes." But I'm just not patient enough to do that. You'll notice that the really great hitters all have that patience, and they all get a lot of walks.

JEFF BURROUGHS: It's not that there's much of a difference between the American and National Leagues, it's just that there seem to be more veteran pitchers in the National, and I like that. I have very poor luck against people I see for the first time.

37

BOB BAILOR: I'm a free swinger and I don't walk or strike out very much. I could be more selective I suppose and only swing at strikes, but that would cut into my aggressive traits, and I'm happy the way I am.

TED SIMMONS: As a catcher, I see baseball as a cat-and-mouse game between the pitcher, the hitter, and the catcher. When I'm at bat, I carry that concept with me. So I think it's an advantage to be a catcher if you keep your mind in that direction.

ROY WHITE: If you're a switch-hitter, the zone may appear different from different sides of the plate. Learn each one independently, and never find yourself saying, "that would have been a strike if I'd been hitting left-handed."

11.

Meeting the Ball

Everything about this book relates to meeting the ball. As you might guess, it's not as easy as it might appear. Some of the best hitters in history have struck out a lot—hitters like Babe Ruth, Mickey Mantle, Lou Brock, and Eddie Mathews. But when they meet the ball, they do it just right.

EDDIE MURRAY: I'm very aggressive. I get in trouble when I overstride. I try to meet the ball when it's right in front of me. If I'm a little late and hit it even with me or a little behind me, I just won't hit it well.

JIM SUNDBERG: It's the toughest thing in all sports—hitting a round ball with a round bat and hitting it squarely. The key is to meet the ball crisp and hard. A fraction of an inch is the difference between a pop up and a liner off the wall.

BOB WATSON: You have to see the ball well. Don't try to overpower it, just wait as long as possible and react accordingly.

HAL McRAE: The main thing is just to relax without overswinging. Keep your head still.

DAVE REVERING: Just hit the ball hard where it's pitched, and you'll get your hits.

ERIC SODERHOLM: It's the hardest thing to do in sports. Just concentrate on seeing the ball leave the bat and don't pull your head away.

JERRY REMY: When you're seeing the ball good—and that's the whole secret to meeting it properly—it'll look like a watermelon. When you're not, it comes in like a BB. You've got to hit down, or at least I do. That's how I make my money!

LOU PINIELLA: It's so tough to do this right. The ball is curving, sliding, knuckling, or what have you, and, of course, the pitcher knows what he's throwing—you don't.

BOBBY MURCER: It's a matter of timing and concentration, but the whole difference between success and failure is just measured in eighths of inches.

Chicago Cubs

BILL ROBINSON: You've got to hit down on a baseball. Hit on top of it and drive through it. Try to always keep that ball in play, and you'll wind up ahead of the game.

JEFF BURROUGHS: I'm really like a golfer up at the plate doing whatever happens to be working for me at the time and adjusting to the situation. You've got to be flexible.

Bobby Murcer knows that it's only a matter of a fraction of an inch that determines whether you meet the ball well or not.

12.

Being Aggressive at the Plate

To be aggressive is to be successful. The best hitters always look as though they're attacking the ball. Watch most pitchers come to bat in the National League. They often feel they won't do well and notice how different they look swinging the bat—not very aggressive at all.

SAL BANDO: I'm always thinking aggressively at the plate. I get my share of walks only because the pitchers have come to respect me. But given the choice, I'd always prefer to swing the bat. When you've been in the league a long time, you get to know the pitchers and can wait for your pitch. It may make you look less aggressive, but you're really not.

AL OLIVER: Being aggressive is more mental than physical to me. The key is the power of positive thinking. I don't try to outthink myself—I just want to see the ball and react to it. I don't look for any particular pitch either. I'm quick enough, fortunately, to get around when and if I'm fooled.

JIM SUNDBERG: I struggled for a few years before I became more selective, and that's when I became

Sal Bando knows that waiting for the pitch does not make you any less aggressive a hitter.

more aggressive. The mental part is so important. You have to be able to tell yourself, "I know I can do it!"

ERIC SODERHOLM: I've really worked at this aspect of the game—worked at it through hypnosis, in fact. It's all mental, and hypnosis has really helped me become more aggressive.

HAL McRAE: I'd say it's mostly mental. At the major league level, almost everyone has the same physical ability. The difference comes in the mental part.

BOBBY MURCER: Baseball is 75 percent mental. The pitchers are always trying to antagonize you and intimidate you. Overcome that and you're on the way to being aggressive at the plate.

LOU PINIELLA: I like to hit to all fields, so I don't have to look out for one particular pitch. And I'm always swinging because I don't like to fall behind on the count and give the pitcher the edge.

JERRY REMY: Aggression at the plate is just a lack of patience in my case. I know I should try to get more walks, but I'd rather be swinging.

JOHN MILNER: Baseball's like a chess game. You've got to know all the moves, and you've got to try to determine each other's weaknesses. When you think you've got the pitcher figured out, that's the time to get aggressive.

JEFF BURROUGHS: While it's true that baseball is very mental, you've got to be able to transfer the mental part to the physical part. I have to keep reminding myself to be aggressive, and when I am, that's when I'm hitting the pitcher's best pitches. If you're aggressive, you'll get a lot more accidental hits too, like those bloops over the infield.

TED SIMMONS: You need aggression to get up to the plate. If you don't have it—if you don't have that attitude—there's no way you'll ever hit consistently.

ROY WHITE: Don't think defensively unless you've got two strikes and are just trying to foul pitches off until you get your pitch. But take advantage of those first two strikes—they're your pitches to do with what you wish, and make the most of them!

13.

Advancing Runners Along

Winning games takes the cooperation of everyone in the lineup. There are times a batter will be called upon to hit behind a runner to move him into scoring position. This usually means hitting the ball toward first or second base with a runner on first—it almost always gets the base runner to second and in position to score on a single to the outfield.

Of course, this strategy usually means that the batter is out, and he doesn't even get a sacrifice recorded for his efforts. But this play is important and is meant to build runs and win games, and only a selfish player or one specifically ordered to swing for a home run will avoid this important part of the game.

DAVE CASH: One of the benefits of the new multi-year contracts is that it's easier for a player to give himself up for the team. You don't have to think about losing a point on your batting average.

AL OLIVER: Give me an inside pitch in these situations and I'll pull it and get the runner over. Of course, the pitcher knows this, so he's trying to keep the ball away from me. It might even force me to bunt instead. But I'm waiting for him to make a mistake.

EDDIE MURRAY: I know I can hit behind a runner, but the way the Orioles are set up now, they don't want me giving myself up. I'm usually ordered to swing away even in those situations. Someday, of course, it could change and I'll be ready.

BUTCH WYNEGAR: Gene Mauch, the Twins' manager, is a great advocate of moving runners up. Sure you're charged with an out, but Gene'll usually make it up to you at another time. I'll tell you this, though—hitting behind a runner isn't something that comes naturally. You've really got to concentrate and work on it.

HAL McRAE: This isn't as much pressure as others think. It's a lot tougher to be in a position to have to drive a run in. Hitting behind a runner calls on you to make an out, and I've done that plenty of times over the years!

ERIC SODERHOLM: I don't do this very well. But you can't worry about hitting the ball to the right side. You've got to take your natural swing, and if the pitch is up the middle, or for me, outside, it should go to the right side of the field.

BOB WATSON: This isn't that hard for me because I'm not a pull hitter. I've learned to do this because I played so long in the Astrodome instead of in a ball park like Atlanta or Chicago, where I might have become more of a power hitter.

LOU PINIELLA: Choke up a little bit if you want to get those runners over. It'll give you much better bat control. But make darn sure you don't swing at an inside pitch (if you're right-handed, outside if you're lefty). Wait for the right pitch!

BILL ROBINSON: Moving the runners is an art, and to get it right, do it in practice, pretending there's a man on first or second. Familiarize yourself with the situation.

JEFF BURROUGHS: I'm not usually called upon to move runners along so much as I am to bring them home. I love those situations. I've always hit better with men on base. Give up the power a little, just get those base hits, and keep those men moving around the bases.

TED SIMMONS: As far as giving yourself up, that's not hard to deal with at all. You're helping to contribute to a winning cause. It can sometimes take a while to realize that this is what the game is all about. But when you help the team, you've helped yourself.

ROY WHITE: I've been fortunate enough to have been fairly successful at hitting behind a runner over the years, and it's helped me become more of a complete player. If you play regularly, you'll have so many times at bat that giving yourself up now and then to move a runner won't really affect your batting average, and the main idea is to help the team.

14.

Going with the Pitch

Hall of Famer Willie Keeler used to explain his batting success by saying, "I just hit 'em where they ain't!" What Willie was saying more than half a century ago still holds true today: The best hitters are the ones who take each pitch and hit it in the right direction for that particular delivery. It means taking an inside pitch and pulling it, taking an outside pitch and going the other way, or taking a pitch over the middle and hitting it straight up the middle of the field.

DAVE CASH: You've really got to try to be quick if the ball's on the inside half of the plate. That's where the quick reaction time comes in. If it's down the middle of the plate, hit it up the middle of the field. And if it's on the outer part of the plate, go to the opposite field with it. You've got to think fast and know the strike zone, of course. Especially with two strikes because that's the "pitcher's pitch"—he's in command.

SAL BANDO: I try to hit the ball when it's *on* the plate, not in front of it. I'll wait, stay back, and try to drive it the opposite way.

JIM SUNDBERG: I hit best when I'm hitting the ball within thirty feet of second base, either side. I look for a ball down the middle of the plate for that. Sooner or later, it usually has to come. I try to "inside-out" pitchers to right field. There's a lot of wrist action in that. When I'm doing that well, I'm at my best.

BOB WATSON: Going with the pitch seems to come naturally to me. I divide the plate in half and look for a ball away—thinking to myself, "Go up the middle." If someone's a dead-pull hitter, it's a lot tougher for him to adjust to a pitch. I've made a good living going with pitches. It's tougher to defense me and pitch me.

DAVE REVERING: Scouts at first shied away from me because I wasn't a pull hitter. Then, in the Cincinnati organization, they converted me to a pull hitter. Now I've decided to relearn it the other way and go with the pitch again.

HAL McRAE: I was taught to stay behind the ball and hit it a little late. Going with the pitch is really necessary today because so many top relief pitchers come in and throw trick pitches to you.

BOBBY MURCER: You can't pull an outside pitch. I should know because I've sure tried it enough. When I want to go to the opposite field, I choke up a little and just punch it out there.

BILL ROBINSON: If I try to pull an outside pitch, I'm just going to ground out weakly.

JERRY REMY: Someday I may reach the point where I want to pull the ball more often, but for now, I'm always thinking "Go the other way." I rely on my legs for a lot of hits, and this helps me.

LOU PINIELLA: Going with the pitch involves the arms and shoulders more than the hands. I keep my hip closed—that is, pointing toward the pitcher—and throw the bat out at the ball. It's a matter of hitting it where it's pitched, and it's the best way to be a successful hitter.

JOHN MILNER: If the ball is on the inside part of the plate and is a strike, hit it out in front of you to pull it. If it's on the outside part of the plate, wait until it's three or four inches from the back of the plate and slam it up the middle. That's how you get the job done.

BOB BAILOR: I bat second in our lineup, so going with the pitch is something I have to do a lot. When you're doing it properly, you find your batting average moving up, because you get the best part of the bat on the ball more often.

TED SIMMONS: I like the high pitches, but with two strikes and, say, men on second and third, I won't get that pitch. So if I'm still planning on pulling the ball, I'm wasting everyone's time. I've got to adjust and go with the pitch, even to the opposite field.

ROY WHITE: Patience is the key here. If you guess breaking ball, and that's what's thrown, make sure you follow up with the necessary patience to meet it correctly. Guessing right and failing is a real disappointment.

Roy White feels that patience is the key to success.

15.

Hitting for Power

Usually the big strong hitters are the ones who hit all the home runs. But sometimes a man can fool you—Ernie Banks, for one, or even Mickey Rivers. They hit more home runs than it looks like they can, and they usually get the extra strength from the wrists. But most hitters will tell you it's all good timing. You can't *try* to hit a home run.

SAL BANDO: It's really tough to accomplish when you're trying. You're usually just blessed with the gift to hit the long ball. But if you can help yourself at all, look for a pitch a little inside and wait until it's on the middle of the plate. Those seem to be easier to hit out. All you can do is hope the pitcher makes a mistake, and be ready for it.

DAVE CASH: A guy that has the ability to hit home runs should just try to meet the ball and the home runs will come. When you intentionally muscle-up, you'll make mistakes.

ERIC SODERHOLM: You've got to be able to see the ball leave the bat and get a good follow-through. The wrists are just an end result of getting your strength from the thighs, hips, chest, and abdominal muscles. To help me, I work with weights a lot.

52

Lou Piniella thinks he could hit ten to fifteen more homers in a smaller ball park, but he adjusts to handle bigger ball parks and gives up power.

HAL McRAE: The home runs will come. It's not how hard you swing, but your bat speed. You can swing for homers on certain pitches, but you better be disciplined enough to wait for that pitch.

BOB WATSON: In the Astrodome, home runs are scarce, so I had to get them out of my mind at home. They come if you just make good contact. Dave Kingman is about the only guy I know who really tries to hit home runs. Not even Mike Schmidt tries.

LOU PINIELLA: Reggie Jackson is one of the few guys who can actually think home run and produce. Generally, it's all a matter of timing, proper weight shift, and getting the ball in the right location—all coming together at once. And, of course, the ball park

New York Yankees

helps. I'd hit ten to fifteen more homers a year in Boston or Detroit than I do in New York.

BILL ROBINSON: Reggie Jackson's the only guy I know who seems to try for a homer every time. When the rest of us try, we're pulling our heads, taking our eyes off the ball, and tightening our muscles. And you've got to maintain the hand-eye coordination.

JERRY REMY: Know your capabilities. I could hit ten home runs a year if I wanted my average to drop to .220. I get into trouble when I try to play long ball.

TED SIMMONS: Look for the ball down the middle of the plate, perhaps a little inside. That's the pitch to hit far. The chances are you'll pull it if you hit it right, and as everyone knows, the shortest distances in a park are right down the lines.

JEFF BURROUGHS: Just don't take your eye off the ball. Wait for the pitcher to make a mistake and try to make really solid contact. You know, home-run streaks, like hitting four or five in a week, are not so much your own doing as just the luck of having pitchers make a lot of mistakes in a short period of time.

BOB BAILOR: I'm hardly an authority on power hitting, but I'll tell you this: one year I hit a home run in the thirteenth inning to win a game. If nothing else, that proves that most home runs are accidents.

JOHN MILNER: Never break your concentration and try to hit the ball hard. That should make it happen. But you can't tell yourself, "Hit a home run." For me, every time I hit one out I still say to myself, "How'd I do that?"

16.

Bunting

Some people say that bunting is a lost art. Many years ago, before power hitting became so popular, teams often bunted, trying to build runs one at a time. Today, only a few craftsmen are considered expert bunters, and many players never even work at improving. But you can still see games won and lost on the ability to bunt correctly or not.

AL OLIVER: I think the whole key to good bunting is to make sure the ball goes down the line—either the first or third base lines.

BUTCH WYNEGAR: I'm not very speedy, so bunting to me is always just a sacrifice, never a hit. All I do is just square around and try to get a piece of the ball.

JIM SUNDBERG: Most guys don't even practice bunting, but you've really got to work at it. I first started taking it seriously when Billy Martin was my manager. I tried the suicide squeeze ten times that year—when you've got to do it right—and I think I was successful all ten times. I'll bet in my career I'm about 20 for 22 or so. Practice really pays off.

DAVE CASH: It's a lot harder than hitting to me. You've got to try to catch the ball with the bat very gently. Make your hands as soft as possible, especially on artificial grass.

ERIC SODERHOLM: It's trying to catch the ball with the bat. You're doing it right when you don't hear much noise when the bat and ball meet. When Carew bunts, you can't hear a thing. It's as though he missed it altogether.

HAL McRAE: Bunting's not that hard to do; it's just not done that much these days. Make sure you have the bat head above the ball and bunt down. Get your hands out in front, but make sure you take the pitch if the ball's above the center of the bat or you'll pop it up.

BOBBY MURCER: I've become a better than average bunter, and I'll almost always bunt for a base hit rather than a sacrifice. I try to keep the bunt near the line so that it'll either be perfect or go foul. I don't want to pop it up. It's all a matter of bat control.

JERRY REMY: Drag bunting is my biggest asset. When you're in a slump you can always bunt your way out of it, if you're good at it. That's a great tool to have.

LOU PINIELLA: Face the pitcher—don't be fancy and rotate on your toes if sacrifice is what you're trying to do. Choke up and keep the top part of the bat above your hands to avoid pop ups. It's really not as hard as some players make it look.

BILL ROBINSON: Good bunting can add ten to fifteen points to a guy's batting average. And if you fake a bunt, you force the infielders in a step or two. Baseball is a game of inches, and those steps could help you drive a base hit through them on the next pitch.

TED SIMMONS: Anyone should be able to learn sacrifice bunting. But bunting for hits, that's a real art. It's very difficult, and it takes a lot of work.

BOB BAILOR: Artificial turf really hurts the bunting game. It's hard to bring the ball to a stop, to deaden it. That's one of the reasons it's probably a lost art.

JOHN MILNER: The main thing is to deaden the ball. But I'm sure glad I'm not asked to bunt very often. It's really tough.

ROY WHITE: Bunting might look easy, but few things require so much practice. It's an art that's ignored by too many players, and it can win a lot of games for you.

17.

Serving as Designated Hitter

The introduction of the designated hitter in 1973 is considered one of the biggest rule changes in the entire history of baseball. Suddenly, pitchers didn't have to bat anymore, and hitters could bat three or four times a game and never play the field. Only the American League adopted it.

The rule gave aging stars a chance to play a little longer, but by no means did serving as designated hitter turn into an easy job. Batting without playing the field required a whole new kind of concentration.

SAL BANDO: I take a heavier bat and swing it in the clubhouse between times at bat, just to stay strong and keep loose. I'll look in the mirror as I swing or even use a tee and whack a wiffle ball around the clubhouse. I run up and down the runway to the dugout. You've got to keep moving.

EDDIE MURRAY: I did it often in my rookie year because it gave me more time to sit on the bench and study pitchers. The hardest part is just keeping loose. I'm always running to the clubhouse, watching the game on the television, or swinging a bat. When you don't hit the ball hard, you really feel bad because you can't go out and help the team defensively.

Hal McRae has adjusted to the role of designated hitter by remembering to keep moving so he won't tighten up during a game.

DAVE CASH: We don't have it in the National League, of course, but it would help a guy like me who hits leadoff. Now, I'm always hitting behind the pitcher except in the first inning. With a DH, I'd hit behind better hitters. As for being a DH myself, I don't think I could handle it now.

HAL McRAE: I've adjusted to it. Only when I'm in a slump do I wish I could play the field, because if you're not hitting, you've got only negatives on your

Kansas City Royals

mind. The important thing is to try and maintain a sweat. Stretch a lot, move around a lot. Don't sit down or you'll tighten up. You can't really watch the game very much. Stay in it mentally, but don't sit down and watch it. Keep moving!

DAVE REVERING: The couple of times I did it I was bored. My mind wandered. I'd really have to make a big adjustment to it.

LOU PINIELLA: If you've had some bad swings, work to correct it in the clubhouse. Obviously, all you've got to do on a day you're the DH is think about hitting.

BOB BAILOR: Veterans seem to be better designated hitters. They're probably less nervous. I get too nervous to be good at it. Rico Carty is always happy-go-lucky—he seems to have the perfect attitude.

ROY WHITE: I've done this off and on over the years but I've never been happy with it. I'm too involved in a game to occupy the time between at bats, usually some thirty-five to forty minutes. I don't know if the rulemakers fully appreciated how hard a job this would be.

18.

Pinch Hitting

The pinch hitter only gets one chance, and he's usually called upon without much time to get ready. It's a difficult assignment, and only a few people have been successful, year after year, as pinch hitters.

JIM SUNDBERG: The adrenaline really flows through your body when you're called up to pinch-hit. I'm usually in the bullpen when I'm called. You don't have time to get nervous, so in a way, it's a little easier than being a designated hitter. But you've got to relax yourself in a hurry.

ROY WHITE: You have no idea how much respect a player gets from other players when he can deliver a key pinch hit. Everyone who's ever done it knows how difficult it is. Try to anticipate when you might be called upon, and begin preparing yourself mentally for action as though you've been in the game right along.

DAVE CASH: It's a very pressurized situation. These guys who do it never get enough credit; they always seem to be overlooked. You couldn't win without them.

HAL McRAE: It's a really difficult job. At Cincinnati, I did a fairly good job because they told me to just go up, get three swings, and don't worry about it. That helped me to relax.

ERIC SODERHOLM: When I first came up and the manager said, "Soderholm, pinch-hit!" my heart would drop to my feet. But experience is the best teacher, and it gets better as you go along.

BOB WATSON: Pinch hitting starts from the first pitch of the game. You must be in the game all the time. Every few innings, get up and swing a bat. Keep asking guys, "what's he throwing, what's he throwing. . . ." If you're mentally prepared, it's a whole lot easier.

LOU PINIELLA: You've got two types of pinch hitters: Those who take the big swing and can win a game for you with a home run, and the more disciplined hitter who always makes contact. The consistent hitter will beat you in a lot of different ways, and he'll probably be around much longer.

BOBBY MURCER: I've only pinch-hit a few times in my career, and I'm happy about that. It's the toughest thing in baseball.

BILL ROBINSON: What a thankless job! The key is to start swinging from the time you get off the bench and don't take too many pitches. You've got to make contact. A guy who misses a lot of pitches won't ever be successful.

TED SIMMONS: It's important to start getting loose early and to think, "Who's the pitcher likely to be if I'm called upon? How should I approach him?"

JOHN MILNER: The best advice for a pinch hitter is to just try to drive the ball hard somewhere.

19.

Studying Statistics

Baseball is a game of numbers. The fans, the press, and just about everyone seem to love keeping up on batting averages, home runs, runs batted in—you name it. But the players probably pay the least attention of all. Or, at least, they make that claim. Who really knows if they sneak a look at the morning paper to see what they're batting?

AL OLIVER: I just try to improve my stats from one season to the next. I've come close to a few batting championships, and one of these days I'm going to win one.

EDDIE MURRAY: I look at statistics because I want to improve every year. Stats are one way for some people to judge players, particularly people who don't get to watch the men day in and day out on the field.

SAL BANDO: Statistics, to me, are very misleading. If you just play to win play for the team to the best of your ability, you'll end up having a good year, and the statistics will take care of themselves.

DAVE CASH: Statistics don't always tell the whole story, but I will admit that in some cases they can be very important. They obviously mean more to players without long-term contracts because those guys have to renegotiate based on the statistics they've compiled.

JIM SUNDBERG: I don't follow them at all. I have no idea how many doubles or triples I had last year.

The true value of a player is realized by observing someone over a full year. I think writers, when they vote for award winners, put too much emphasis on statistics.

ERIC SODERHOLM: I do study statistics because I'm very goal-oriented. I like to set short-term goals for myself, like how many hits will I get this week, and I keep up on my stats, hoping the short-term goals will expand into long-term ones.

HAL McRAE: The bottom line is winning. I like to have good stats, but I'm not very involved with them.

BOB WATSON: Statistics have their place, but really, some guys can drive in a hundred runs, and maybe only fifteen or twenty were really important ones. That's where the misleading part comes in.

LOU PINIELLA: Statistics are good for the game— they're always a source of conversation, and the fans like to follow them. While they don't measure total value, you really can't hide them if you're not doing a good job.

BOBBY MURCER: Year-to-year stats don't mean much to me. A five-year compilation shows me a lot more. If a guy's done such and such over a five-year period, you really know what you've got in a player. After just a couple of years, it's hard to predict what he can do for you.

JEFF BURROUGHS: Statistics are great! They're great for baseball and great for the fans. I think everyone follows his own stats. It's a prideful thing.

20.

Great Hitters on Hitting

Two of the most dedicated hitters in the history of baseball had to be Ted Williams and Harry Walker. Either of them would talk hitting at any time, in any place, or in any company. When they talked about hitting, they became completely absorbed in the subject.

There is no end to stories about Williams and his dedication to the science of hitting. For example, there was one pitcher in the American League who had given Ted a lot of trouble. One day the Red Sox acquired the pitcher in a trade and, a short time afterward, Ted got the pitcher to throw him some extra batting practice. "If he gets traded to another club, he'll never get me out," said Ted after the BP session in which he figured out why the pitcher had been successful against him.

There are no ifs, ands, or buts in Williams' theories. He expounds them as gospel truths. Some of those things that remained in the listeners' minds—whether ballplayers or not—were the following:

1. *Never swing at a pitch you can't reach comfortably.*
2. *Every time you go to bat you'll get your pitch at least once–be ready for it.*

3. Don't be afraid to take two strikes to get your pitch.
4. Be patient.

Williams, of course, had the aura of greatness about him that made him the oracle of hitting. Harry Walker didn't command that much awe, yet his hitting theories were also effective, and he helped many players improve at bat.

Harry basically tried to adjust the hitter's batting to his size and ability. He didn't worry about distance, but merely getting hits, and that's what he taught— bunt, chop down on the ball, and find the holes.

Walker readily admits that he learned early that he couldn't hit the ball out of the park. Instead, he taught himself to hit for average. He used every trick in the book, and in 1947 won the National League batting title with a .363 mark.

Oddly enough, Walker started that year with St. Louis and was traded to the Phillies. He had 186 hits, of which 140 were singles and only 1 was a home run. In fact, Harry hit only 10 homers in 2,651 times at bat. He proved, however, that you don't have to hit the ball out of the park to be a good hitter, and he wound up with a .296 career average.

Harry Walker was part of the only brother combination to both win batting championships. Dixie won his in 1944 at .357 with the Dodgers. Dixie Walker played eighteen years and had a career mark of .306. He was a batting instructor for the Dodgers until he retired in 1977 when he was sixty-seven.

The Walker brothers both served many years as batting instructors. Dixie had more power than Harry, but both had picture swings and were disciplined hitters.

Remember the Hawk? That, of course, is Ken Harrelson, who is now a TV commentator in Boston. Harrelson was one of the first players to break away from his team and sign for big numbers. In 1967 he became a celebrity when Charlie Finley gave Harrelson his unconditional release. He then signed with Boston.

Ken has a lot of thoughts on hitting and hitters and how the game has changed. In fact, he goes out on his own with the theory that the biggest change in hitters is pitchers. That might sound strange without his explanation.

Harrelson bases his theory on how few pitchers go nine innings today. In today's baseball, a hitter is liable to face four pitchers, rarely facing a tired pitcher. In addition, today's hurlers are likely to throw anything on 3-0 or 3-2 counts, not the fastball that once was automatic.

Ken agrees with Luis Arroyo that hitters are beginning to get away from the home-run syndrome. He believes hitters are getting smarter because they are receiving better coaching in high school and college.

The more hitters you talk to about their expertise, the more ideas you uncover. Ken, for example, discussed the amount of time a hitter sees the ball as it travels from pitcher to the plate. He claims that Rod Carew sees the ball for 60½ feet, then adds that Thurman Munson was one of the ten best hitters he had ever seen. Harrelson claims that when Munson, who had great concentration, was on a hot streak, he saw the ball for 60½ feet. Harrelson's observation was confirmed by Munson. Any hitting streak by Munson inevitably brought the comment, "I'm seeing the ball great."

Harrelson, on the other hand, figured the best he

could do was see the ball 52 feet and said that greater concentration added 2 feet to the pitcher's fastball. Ken has a few batting tips for you, too. He advises you not to try to cover the entire plate, but make sure you cover part of it.

Ken warns against trying to cover the whole plate to battle top pitchers such as Ron Guidry, Luis Tiant, and Jim Palmer. Against the top pitcher, the hitter must do the best he can and be ready to jump on any mistake the pitcher might make.

The Hawk feels that batting coaches can help hitters if the hitters will let them. He warns against batting coaches who try to make a hitter in his own image rather than improving what the hitter has. Here's good news for all of you having trouble at bat: Ken is convinced that a poor hitter can be improved considerably with good coaching and hard work.

21.

Pitchers Talk Hitting

If hitters spend a lot of time talking about pitching, it stands to reason that the man on "the other end of the gun" spends considerable time talking about hitters.

In trying to instruct you in all the details of hitting, it would seem logical to include a chapter on how a pitcher thinks in relation to the hitters. Naturally, each hitter must follow his own dictates as to how intent he will be on pitchers.

To Whitey Ford, Hall of Fame left-hander, the hitter-versus-pitcher battle is strictly a guessing game. The longer the pair oppose each other, the tougher the battle becomes, and it does add a lot of spice to the game.

Ford, who was always a shrewd individual, actually cataloged the hitters into different categories. He still remembers that Harvey Kuenn and the late Nellie Fox were two of the toughest hitters he ever faced. They were tough to fool, had a short stroke, and rarely struck out. Each time either one came to bat it was a battle.

Ford's favorite category was the hitters who never change. They do the same thing from their first day to the last, making them the smart pitcher's friends. In some instances, these hitters are just stubborn enough to keep doing the same thing in hope of winning, but they never do.

Whitey Ford was considered the craftiest of modern pitchers, employing a large variety of pitches to keep hitters off balance.

Whitey had the benefit of advice from another smart left-handed pitcher, Eddie Lopat. When they sat together on the bench during games, Lopat would point out things that Ford absorbed and turned to his use. Lopat, of course, had many different speeds and body movements that helped him control the hitters.

Whitey points out that the biggest change in hitters while he was in the majors was the gradual move to power. Even the little guys had slim bat handles and tried to knock the ball out of the park. It seemed that the smart hitter was fading out as everyone went home-run crazy.

Stan Williams was more of a power pitcher for the Dodgers, Yankees, Indians, and Twins in a lengthy career. He has also been a minor league manager and a major league pitching coach—all of which qualifies him as an authority.

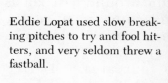

Eddie Lopat used slow breaking pitches to try and fool hitters, and very seldom threw a fastball.

New York Yankees

Any major league pitcher, according to Williams, has the ability to get a batter out, but the difference between throwers and pitchers is in observation. A pitcher anxious to improve will sit on the bench watching the opposing team take batting practice. He can watch how the various hitters, especially newcomers, go into the ball and watch the front shoulder for telltale signs. If a hitter holds the bat straight up he is probably a low ball hitter. Watch the hitter's reactions at the moment the pitcher starts his delivery, for example. Does he try to lure the pitcher into thinking incorrectly?

Williams says that the major change he has seen in the last few years is the growth of guess hitters. Stan believes that the hitters are always trying to outguess the pitchers and that is the pitcher's edge. The man with the ball always has an edge in a guessing game—a pitcher, a quarterback, or what have you. Williams also feels that hitters have helped pitchers by becoming long ball conscious.

Luis Arroyo has been bouncing around baseball as a pitcher, scout, manager, and club executive for many years. He has seen hitters from all angles and come up with some ideas of his own.

He categorized hitters into four areas: (1) free swingers, (2) go with the pitch, (3) Punch and Judy, and (4) guess hitters. He puts most of the long-ball hitters in the latter category, and he really liked to face them.

Pitching in his native Puerto Rico as well as in the United States, Luis saw all types of hitters. When he came into a new league or a new hitter appeared, Arroyo would check him out for size, where he stood at the plate, whether he was a free swinger or a smart hitter, how he held the bat, and how quick his bat was. Luis warns to watch out for hitters with a quick bat.

Al Kaline is Arroyo's choice as his toughest rival because he never guessed; he just hit the ball where it was pitched. All pitchers love to watch guess hitters and those who never try to adjust no matter how often a pitcher gets them out. Luis did express the opinion that in the past few years he has seen more hitters starting to go with the pitch and stop guessing.

Bob Lemon started as an outfielder before moving to pitcher. He remained one of the best hitting pitchers in baseball, and used his batting knowledge to develop into a Hall of Fame pitcher for the Cleveland Indians.

Bob Lemon, the Hall of Fame star, was a plain pitcher with no frills. Therefore, it is not surprising that he had the same attitude when talking about hitters. His basic principal was to be careful of the long-ball hitters and not worry about the other guys, since they can't hurt you that much.

When ball clubs have meetings to go over opposing hitters, the principal idea is to learn what they can't hit, unless you are Lemon or are playing for him. He doesn't worry about what they can't hit, he wants to know about what they can hit so you can match strength to strength. Lemon figures he is using logic to devise that system since if he learns that a hitter is a good low-ball hitter and he (Bob) is a high-ball pitcher, there's nothing he can do about it.

Like all pitchers, Lemon studies the hitters, but he takes a little different viewpoint. His system is to watch if the hitter makes any changes or adjustments in his stance or grip. If he does, then it is a good bet that you can't get him out the way you did last time.

In facing a hitter for the first time, Bob's system is simple once again—throw him your best stuff. By the second time around the league, pitchers have a good picture of any new hitter.

Another bit of advice that the Hall of Famer passes along is the power of positive thinking. A pitcher must never think negatively, no matter how often any hitter has belted him in the past. Each new confrontation must find the pitcher thinking positive thoughts.

Like all pitchers, Lemon says that concentration is a very important part of any pitcher's equipment. If your mind isn't on your work, you'll do a bad job no matter what your work happens to be. Another "must" is to stay ahead of the hitter since that gives the pitcher an edge. Don't overthrow is another bit of advice.

Lemon also pointed out that it is a rare day when a pitcher goes into a game and finds all of his pitches working well. He says that when those days come along, you have no worries, since the hitters can't touch you. Usually, however, the first order of business is to establish which of your pitches is best that day and use it for your out pitch.

Pitchers discussing their craft—a good way to learn hitting in reverse!

22.

Tips from a
Home-Run King

Roger Maris was always his own man, which could be one reason why the holder of the single-season home-run record has different ideas about hitting. Possessor of one of the most perfectly level swings ever seen, Maris starts from a point not previously mentioned. In keeping with his individuality, Roger admits that his basic comment on giving hitting tips might sound silly: Build up your wrists! That's Maris' opening bit of advice to any of you hoping to be a good hitter.

Maris explains that a wrist hitter has many advantages over a nonwrist hitter. The primary edge is the ability to wait longer before committing himself to swing at any pitch. This, of course, is a big advantage against a breaking-ball pitcher. A free swinger often gets too far out in front of the pitch from finesse pitchers.

Roger Maris won two Most Valuable Player awards and played in seven World Series. He is best remembered for his record breaking 61 home runs in 1961.

Roger finds that bat selection is also a most important item. In fact, he believes you should be fitted for a bat almost as you are for a pair of shoes or a jacket. He also warns that this will take time and effort because you have to try out many bats to find the right weight and length that suits your size and strength best.

Maris agrees with those who insist that a batter's stance is a very personal thing that no one can help with. Every hitter, young or old, must find a stance with which he is comfortable, then stick with it. It may look funny or be impossible for your friend, but it's great for you.

How do you know when you find the right stance? It is amazing how quickly you find out. You'll see the ball better, feel comfortable swinging, and enjoy going to bat. There is a word of warning, however—it isn't permanent.

Roger points out that your perfect stance today may be less perfect tomorrow because of several factors. In the first place, you grow bigger and stronger and may find a new stance more comfortable. It is possible, too, that the pitchers will force you into a new stance. If you have a "blind spot," the pitchers will work on it; then you try a new stance to eliminate it.

Once you have found the right bat and matched it with the right stance, find a mirror, preferably a full-length one. Stand in front of it—far enough in front so that you won't break it and go hitless with seven years of bad luck. Now is the time to try and develop a smooth, level swing minus any hitch. Don't chop at the ball or uppercut it as you swing. Keep the bat level and swing smoothly. An uneven swing results in pop ups, and that's no way to build an average.

Who cares how hard you swing? The pitchers love to see that since it gives them an edge. The harder you swing the more ways they have to get you out. If you think the ball travels further when you swing hard, forget it. That's a myth. The secret in getting distance is timing, not hard swings.

What is timing? Boiling it down to basics, it is getting everything into the ball at just the right moment. What is everything? Everything is body, leverage, and power into the ball at the same instance with the perfect point of impact just off the center of the body. Any time your body is ahead of your bat, your timing is off.

Maris was always a realist and attributed his sensational home-run season in 1961, when he hit 61, to ⅛ of an inch. He claimed that in that year he was in a groove where he was hitting the ball ⅛ of an inch lower, enabling him to get height on the ball. He claimed that ⅛ of an inch higher would have resulted in a lot of line-drive doubles, which he hit in 1962.

Moving more into the science of hitting, Maris advises that you learn to use the bat, not just swing it. Hitting can be reduced to a science, and all the top hitters have done just that. They are the ones with the fewest strikeouts, the ones who always get a piece of the ball and become expert hit-and-run men.

If you can really use the bat, then you have an edge. You can use all the space between foul lines, which means you can hit to all fields. You don't care too much whether the pitcher is left- or right-handed, for you are always in control. If you are able to use the bat, the pitcher knows he is in trouble. If you just swing, the pitcher has the edge.

Learn concentration at the plate, and don't let anything distract you. Each time you step into the batter's box, have nothing on your mind but the pitcher and where you are going to try to hit the ball. Keep your eye on the ball at all times. The quicker you can pick it up at the release point, the longer you see it.

When you step into the box you should know what the situation calls for and how many outs are on the board. Sometimes the most important thing for you to do is just to hit to the right side and move runners.

Sometimes a bunt can get the winning run home. If you can pull it off, forget about the fences.

If you hit .400 in Little League or high school, don't think you have it made. Chances are you have a weakness or two. Every hitter has weaknesses so the thing to do is learn what they are and work on them.

It may be impossible to eliminate a weakness, but you can certainly improve in that area. Don't waste time in batting practice trying to see how far you can hit the ball. Use BP to improve yourself. Work on your weakness, try to improve your bunting, and try going to the opposite field. If you are a left-handed hitter, for example, always try to get batting practice against left-handed pitchers. The more lefties you see the better you will hit them.

Roger offers other little tips: (1) Don't get classified or typed by the pitchers (for instance, don't be known as a first-ball hitter); (2) don't be known as a hitter who won't bunt; and (3) keep changing around. Always be aggressive and jump on any pitch that gets away from the pitcher. Always try to stay in control of the situation.

23.

Views from a College Coach

Let's move briefly from the pro ball parks to college and high school diamonds.

Doug Holmquist, who was a minor league catcher, has coached at the high school, junior college, and college levels and has just started a career as a minor league manager. He has written papers on hitting and has tried to teach boys of all ages its intricacies. Here he gives us the picture as seen by a college coach.

Like the others, Doug says that a bat must feel good to a hitter as a prerequisite for a proper selection. Then he brings up a new point. He feels consideration should be taken for the type of hitter making the selection. Dividing hitters into such categories as the hit-and-run hitter, the line-drive hitter aiming for the alleys, and the long-ball hitter who lofts the ball, Holmquist expressed the opinion that there is a bat for each category. It is up to the hitter to find it.

Holmquist puts great faith in a lot of batting practice even during the season. He also stresses observing

Doug Holmquist brought college teaching skills into professional baseball.

the pitcher from the on deck circle. He believes one thing a batter can learn by closely observing the pitcher is how he works his patterns. The first and second hitters in a lineup, who are usually the pesky types of batters, will see a wide variety of pitches in a varied set of locations. In other words, the pitcher is working on this type of hitter. By observing from the on deck circle, you can get a good view of the pitcher's selection of pitches.

The powerful hitters in the third, fourth, and fifth slots are usually good fastball hitters, and that changes the pitching plan. These hitters will see a lot of breaking pitches, but a fastball now and then keeps them on their toes. The fastball will usually be a tough pitch, perhaps high and inside.

In most cases, the bottom four hitters will see a lot of hard stuff, including snapping sliders. Here the pitcher will use the breaking pitch just to showcase it. To this collegiate coach it is a cardinal sin to ever throw a weak hitter off-speed pitches.

Doug believes that the finding of a right stance is predicated on two things: (1) the hitter's ability with relation to velocity and (2) his consistency in handling the breaking pitch. The stance is learned by experience. Striding is given a new terminology when Holmquist says, "The stride should be short (six to ten inches) and soft—stride on egg shells."

Our college instructor naturally talks of keeping your eye on the ball, but you must concentrate on the pitcher from the bench, to the on deck circle, and to the batter's box. Now you need tunnel vision to pick up the ball over the pitcher's throwing shoulder.

It is quite natural that Holmquist believes in the value of coaching. He puts it clearly: "Without coaching from the physical and mental aspects of the game, you are left with only what natural ability you have. It is a meager thing to guide you on the road to success—a great gift, but not totally complete without coaching."

Holmquist recommends use of the batting tee as an aid when you're learning the strike zone. It is advised that the tee be set at various heights, which can show the area covered by a strike zone.

Extension of the arms and quickness are the keys to meeting the ball consistently. Holmquist says aggressiveness is of utmost importance not only in hitting, but in any phase of the game. He doesn't want nonaggressive players, but he wants them always to be aggressive within legal limits.

When bunting, he advocates use of the pivot bunt, not squaring away to get set. The bat should be held at the top of the strike zone and at an upward angle, with the top hand at the label on the bat, the top arm almost totally extended, and a predetermined bat angle.

The designated hitter gets more credit from coaches and managers than most fans give him. All recognize that it takes a certain type of personality to do a good job, primarily because he is not in the flow of the game and must get into it as his turn at bat comes.

The pinch hitter is respected as well, and the job is called one of the toughest in baseball. Doug Holmquist, who is a tough disciplinarian, says a pinch hitter must be a guy with a tough, team-oriented attitude.

There isn't too much difference in how the pro manager and the college coach approach the subject of instructing a hitter. There is a difference in words, but basically they both get to the same points.

24.

Exceptions to Every Theory

It would be natural to assume that such great hitters as Joe DiMaggio, Stan Musial, Babe Ruth, Mel Ott, Yogi Berra, Paul Waner, and the immortal Ty Cobb were all of perfection as hitting stylists. But if the ordinary hitter, or even many professionals, tried to hit as these Hall of Famers did, they would find it impossible. Each of these men had a batting stance suited only to himself and most of their stances were contrary to accepted form and models.

DiMaggio stood quietly with his bat cocked and took only a six-inch stride, but no pitcher could take advantage of that style. He had the height and arm length that enabled him to cover the entire plate without waving the bat or striding. Joe's stance was most unusual, but he had great advantages because the shorter the stride, the easier it is to keep your eye level on the ball.

Al Simmons had a .334 lifetime average for twenty seasons in the majors, but a perfectionist scouting him may have refused to sign him. Al performed what is supposedly called the "kiss of death" for any hitter—he "stepped into the bucket." Simmons, who drove in 1,827 runs and hit 307 homers, was a devastating right-handed hitter, but as he stepped into the ball, his left foot went toward third base, not the mound. Al had the equalizer for his unorthodox style—size and strength. As Al got ready to hit, he looked straight at the pitcher and then would step toward third. Al was so powerful that he could still drive the ball with power. His style would not be adaptable to many other players.

Another solo performer was Stan Musial with his corkscrew stance. He looked as if he was so tied up that it would be impossible for him to be a good hitter. But he wasn't just a good hitter—he was great!

When Stan retired after twenty-two years with the Cardinals he held some fifty records and a lifetime batting average of .331. He was second in games played and hits, third in at bats, fifth in runs scored and runs batted in, and sixth in bases on balls. No one has ever batted like Stan the Man, who could overcome his unusual style because of extraordinary eyesight and great reflexes.

Perhaps the most unusual stance of all was Mel Ott's habit of lifting his right foot as the pitcher prepared to release the ball. Lifting his foot enabled him to time the pitch better and stride. Many hitters just slide their foot when they stride, but Ott lifted it high in the air.

Not too many baseball fans are aware of the fact that Paul Waner also lifted his foot as he hit, but not as high as Ott and it wasn't as noticeable. Both Waner and Ott, however, used that to help time the pitches. Although they were fooled at times, the percentage was with them.

Heinie Groh is a name probably few of you reading this book ever heard of. He was an infielder with the New York Giants and used a bat shaped like a bottle. As he stepped into the batter's box, he would be directly facing the pitcher. But as the pitch started, Groh's body turned to first base while keeping his eye on the ball. He spent sixteen years in the majors and had a lifetime .292 average, which is pretty good for an infielder.

Ty Cobb was perhaps the greatest of all and holds first place in more categories than any other player. He is mentioned primarily to point out that he had his hands separated on the bat until he got ready to swing, then he would bring them together. One of his great contemporaries, Tris Speaker, always had his elbows high and the bat over the plate.

Roger Maris had an excellent swing and form, but was unusual in that he did his hitting with his arms and body, not his wrists. That could explain why he was a streak hitter. When his arms and body were not moving together, his swing was off.

Joe Medwick and Yogi Berra were two of the most natural but also the most unorthodox hitters of all. Both had reputations as bad-ball hitters, but they had such a natural swing that they didn't need form. It has been said that Yogi's bat was always in position to swing.

How about Babe Ruth? He had the most unusual stance of all and no one could ever duplicate it. He would stand with his back to the pitcher and would have a longer distance to swing the bat than any other hitter and also the heaviest bat. Babe compensated for

Babe Ruth was voted the Greatest Player Ever by a national poll conducted in 1969. He revolutionized hitting by introducing the concept of home runs to the daily offense.

the long sweep with tremendous wrist power and bat speed. He had perfect timing and probably never had a lesson in his life.

To conclude, here's a story that typifies how the Babe felt about rules, regulations, and theories.

In the spring of 1932, George Selkirk, who was destined to replace Ruth in 1935, was a rookie in spring training. Standing in the outfield with Ruth, Selkirk moaned, "I feel terrible at bat. My feet are terrible, my hands are tight, and my stance is off."

"Son," Ruth began, "that's what is wrong with all you kids. You worry too much about stance, grip, bat, and everything else. All you have to do is keep your head still and your eye on the ball—then hit it."

"I never listened to another bit of advice as long as I played," Selkirk recalls.

25.

You Don't Need Fancy Equipment

Most of today's stars began playing ball in Little Leagues, where instruction was always to be found (some good, some less than good). Bats and balls seemed plentiful, and as youngsters rose higher in the ranks, the mechanics of playing seemed more defined.

Is that what helped to develop today's best hitters? Not really. Listen to Monte Irvin, a member of the Hall of Fame, and a man who had it both ways—the classy major leagues and the rough and tumble Negro Leagues of thirty years ago.

"We never had much in the way of equipment back then," recalled Monte. "A few bats, some balls, and that was it. I remember a club owner going crazy when one of our players on the old Newark Eagles kept hitting foul balls into the stands. 'Would you just strike out and stop wasting those balls?' he would shout!

Monte Irvin, a member of the Hall of Fame, was a star in the Negro Leagues and the National League. He played in two World Series with the New York Giants.

"We didn't have a lot of people around either. There was the manager, one older player who doubled as a coach, and about twenty players. No trainer either. We worked on each other, and the usual cure-all was hot water. We didn't have any of the advanced training methods available to us at all.

"With so few bats around, we learned to take care of what we had. One year, I used just one bat for about two thirds of the season. Seemed as though I never hit it anyplace but on the fat part of the wood. You break bats by getting fooled and hitting it on the handle, but I was having just a great year.

"Spring training wasn't much, either. About two or three weeks in Florida and then we'd head north and play. I don't think you need all the time they devote to it today."

When Monte was thirty, he joined the New York Giants, and the abundance of equipment, trainers, batting machines, and so on impressed him greatly. But he had developed his great hitting skills without their benefit. He was a self-made hitter, and his lesson proves that you can make it on your own.

"One drill I used to think was a big help was just tossing a ball into the air and hitting it. Like hitting fungoes but, of course, using my own bat. It was great for the eye and for timing because you'd try to hit fly balls or line drives or hard grounders, so you would really watch to see that the ball hit the proper part of the bat.

"Playing pepper was a good drill too. It developed quick reflexes and a similar eye-hand coordination. It involves hitting a ball to several players in rapid succession from about twenty-five feet away."

When Irvin played in the Negro Leagues, the players used bats made for major leaguers. Monte

himself used a big Jimmie Foxx model. The idol of all
Negro League players, of course, was the immortal
Josh Gibson.

"Josh had just a perfect swing," recalls Irvin. "Like
Ted Williams, it was picture book perfect. He'd uppercut a little to get that home-run lift on the ball, but
everything about his style was perfection. You can't
just go out and try to copy someone, but he'd be a
great one to start with and then develop your own
style."

Monte also points out that too many hitters today
swing from the heels and look to hit the long ball.
This is especially common among hitters who feel a
fastball, if hit hard, will pop out of the ball park.
That's why the hard throwers like Nolan Ryan and
Ron Guidry have success. If hitters would just try to
knick away at the pitches, says Irvin, they'd have better success. Just get the bat out there, and the velocity
of the ball will cause the bat to send line drives into
the outfield for base hits.

Monte also talked about an old habit that has been
lost to the ages—drawing a line with your foot to show
where you want to step. "It's a great way to avoid
stepping into the bucket," he said. "Draw a line in the
dirt to show where you want to place your foot as
you're striding. It's a great help, but no one bothers
with it anymore."

A common question that youngsters ask, especially
when they watch televised baseball and see the catcher
giving signs, is, "Why doesn't the hitter just look down
to see where the target is?" Well for one thing, the
catcher would see it, even if it was just a glance out of
the corner of his eye. Once the batter returned to face
the pitcher, the catcher could easily move the target,
and it could spell real trouble for the batter. Some-

times, though, a real game goes on involving that target. Some catchers will show a target in one spot, but let the pitcher know with their bare hand to throw to another. Or it will all be arranged beforehand, as though to say, "If the target is here, it means throw here."

One last observation made by Monte Irvin on the nature of baseball today: "In the old days, there seemed to be a natural elimination process for youngsters. If a player was good and had a lot of desire, he'd be out there every day. Sooner or later, the lesser players would fall by the wayside, unable to keep up. So the good players emerged quickly. Today, with the formality of Little Leagues, everyone seems to play equally, and that elimination process doesn't begin until much later."

Conclusion

As we said at the start of this book, hitting is something not everyone agrees on. There are as many different theories around as there are people to go to for advice.

The basics seem to come down to these: Feel comfortable, concentrate, keep your eye on the ball, and be confident. The art of hitting a baseball, one of the most satisfying feelings in sports, will then come to you.

Stars come and go. You may hold onto this book for years and someday look back at the players who shared their thoughts with you and wonder whatever became of them. But one thing is for sure: while they were in the major leagues, they all practiced their skills and learned to enjoy hitting. Baseball is, after all, a game. If it's not enjoyable, you should probably be doing something else. But if you can crack it, if you can have fun and feel comfortable on a baseball field, you're part of the national pastime, and part of one of the continuing rituals of America—whacking a round ball with a round bat and hitting it squarely!